TERRORIST
GROUPS

By Cory Gunderson

VISIT US AT
WWW.ABDOPUB.COM

Published by ABDO & Daughters, an imprint of ABDO Publishing Company, 4940 Viking Drive, Suite 622, Edina, Minnesota 55435.

Printed in the United States.

Edited by: Sheila Rivera
Contributing Editors: Chad Morse, Chris Schafer
Graphic Design: Arturo Leyva, David Bullen
Cover Design: Castaneda Dunham, Inc.
Photos: Corbis

Library of Congress Cataloging-in-Publication Data

Gunderson, Cory Gideon
    Terrorist groups / Cory Gunderson.
      p. cm. -- (World in conflict. The Middle East)
    Includes bibliographical references and index.
    Contents: An overview of terrorism -- Al-Qaeda -- Hamas --Hezbollah --Other Middle East terrorist groups -- Other world terrorist groups.
      ISBN 1-59197-413-5
        1. Terrorists--Middle East--Juvenile literature. 2. Qaida (Organization)--Juvenile literature. 3. arakat al-Muqảwamah al-Islảmayah--Juvenile literature. 4. Hizballah (Lebanon)--Juvenile literature. [1. Terrorists. 2. Terrorism. 3. Qaida (Organization) 4. Hamas. 5. Hizballah (Lebanon)] I. Title. II World in Conflict. Middle East.

    HV6433.M5G85 2003
    303.6'25--dc21

                                                                      200304535

TABLE OF CONTENTS

Taliban soldiers standing alongside a tank in Afghanistan

AN OVERVIEW OF TERRORISM

The word "terrorism" was first coined in the late eighteenth century. Following the French Revolution, every person believed to be an enemy of the new government was executed. The period of time between 1793 and 1794 became known as France's "Reign of Terror." The newly formed French government praised terror as the best way to protect freedom.

Today, experts are clear that the September 11, 2001, attacks against the United States were acts of terrorism. Still, even experts have difficulty coming up with a firm definition of terrorism. The U.S. State Department defines terrorism as "premeditated, politically motivated violence perpetrated against noncombatant targets by subnational groups or clandestine agents, usually intended to influence an audience."

The State Department sets and maintains U.S. foreign policies. Its definition of terrorism can be put into simpler terms. A terrorist group is not an entire country but a subset of people with common goals. Terrorism includes violent acts committed against people who are not soldiers of war. Terrorists secretly plan their actions with the goal to change an existing political order. They are motivated to bring attention to the needs of their group.

Sometimes terrorist groups will even claim responsibility for an attack that they didn't commit. They welcome the attention to their cause that their violence, or even someone else's, brings. Terrorists use shocking displays of violence to scare more than just their victims. They believe that the more people they scare, the better their chances are of getting their demands met. Brian Jenkins, a terrorism expert, states quite simply, "Terrorism is theatre."

The following chapters explain the three major terrorist groups in the Middle East. Other, lesser known, Middle Eastern terrorist groups and terrorist groups from around the globe are also included. What most of these groups have in common is the conviction that they have been wronged.

The aftermath of a terrorist bombing in Jerusalem

Most terrorists also believe in a strict interpretation of their religion. Terrorists are different than more moderate believers within their religion. They are considered extremists, militants, or radicals. Terrorists are so passionate about their group's needs that they are willing to die for their cause.

Middle Eastern women display photos of suicide bombers.

AL-QAEDA

In Arabic, al-Qaeda means "the base." Al-Qaeda is a terrorist network that finances and directs the actions of radical Islamic fundamentalist groups in about 60 countries.

The origins of al-Qaeda came together in Afghanistan in the 1980s. Osama bin Laden is al-Qaeda's founder and leader. Bin Laden is the son of a rich Saudi Arabian businessman. Abdullah Azzam, a religious scholar from Palestine, was in partnership with bin Laden. Together, these men organized a recruiting center called the "Services Office."

It is believed that bin Laden received between 30 and 300 million dollars after his father's death. Bin Laden used his wealth to recruit holy warriors, or mujahedeen, from more than 50 countries. He paid for the holy warriors' transportation to Afghanistan.

A store owner in Karachi, Pakistan, displays Osama bin Laden merchandise.

Most of the mujahedeen were Sunni Muslims. All were eager to defend their fellow Muslims in Afghanistan from the 1979 invasion of the Soviets. The Afghan government gave land and other resources to support the mujahedeen.

The U.S. goal was the same as the mujahedeen at that time. Both groups wanted the Soviet Union out of Afghanistan. During the Soviet invasion, the U.S. government spent about $500 million a year to provide weapons and training to this group. Bin Laden's money was also used to train as many as 10,000 fighters.

After 10 years of fighting, the Soviets were defeated and forced out of Afghanistan. Some of the holy warriors returned to their homelands and resumed the lives they'd left. For others, the mujahedeen victory resulted in the jihad, or holy war, movement. They returned to their homelands feeling passionate about Muslim fundamentalism.

Bin Laden's followers officially took the name al-Qaeda in 1988. Osama continued to use his wealth to fund what became a terrorist group. Al-Qaeda members believe their God, or Allah in Arabic, calls them to defend Islam, even if they must use violence. Al-Qaeda's goals are believed to be:

- The establishment of the rule of Allah on earth.
- The attainment of martyrdom, or the sacrificing of one's life, for the cause of Allah.
- The purification of the ranks of Islam from morally corrupt, or evil, influences.

By 1989, al-Qaeda used the knowledge it gained from its fight against the Soviets to set up terror cells. Terror cells were small groups of al-Qaeda members that helped other extremist Islamic fundamentalists use violence against non-religious Arab governments. Al-Qaeda considered such governments infidels, or nonbelievers in the teachings of the Islamic Prophet Muhammad.

In the early 1990s, al-Qaeda was still in its infant stages of development. The U.S. government had moved its soldiers into Saudi Arabia during the Gulf War. The troops were stationed there to protect Middle East countries and U.S. oil interests from Iraq. The terrorist group began to see the U.S. as an enemy and made a goal to remove it from Saudi Arabia. Muslims consider Saudi Arabia, especially the cities of Mecca and Medina, as holy land.

Al-Qaeda opposed the U.S. because it viewed it as an infidel nation. It felt the U.S. was wrong not to govern its people according to the laws of Islam. Al-Qaeda also hated the U.S. because it provided food, military, and financial support to the Saudi Arabian and Egyptian governments.

Rescue efforts are made after the U.S. Embassy in Nairobi, Kenya, was bombed by Al-Qaeda terrorists.

Bin Laden's group strongly opposed the U.S.'s role in the Gulf War and the war in Somalia. Al-Qaeda felt that in both cases the U.S. was attempting to occupy Arab land and remove a Muslim government. The group also resented the U.S.'s support of Israel because Israel had taken control of what was once Arab land. The U.S. also angered al-Qaeda by jailing its members for crimes of terrorism.

Al-Qaeda's goal came to be the establishment of a pan-Islamic Caliphate system in all Muslim countries. This would place a caliph, or Muslim leader, at the head of every Muslim nation. Al-Qaeda embraces a strict, fundamentalist view of Islam. The group would like all Muslim countries to have this kind of government. Al-Qaeda wants all Muslim nations to be free from Western influences.

Al-Qaeda is believed to be responsible for the bombings of U.S. embassies in Nairobi, Kenya, and Dar es Salaam, Tanzania, in 1998. These attacks killed more than 300 people. More than 5,000 others were hurt.

The terrorist group was also charged with three separate bombings in Aden, Yemen, in December of 1992. In each case, U.S. troops were targeted.

Al-Qaeda's attacks against the U.S. have been the result of a series of fatwahs, or law-like demands. Between 1992 and 1993,

Osama bin Laden issued fatwahs asking Muslims to attack
American military forces in Africa, particularly in Somalia.
He claimed responsibility for the deaths of 18 U.S. servicemen
in Somalia in 1994.

In February 1998, bin Laden called for Muslims to attack
all Americans. He said, "We, with God's help, call on every
Muslim who believes in God and wishes to be rewarded to
comply with God's order to kill the Americans and plunder their
money wherever and whenever they find it...The ruling to kill
the Americans and their allies, civilians and military, is an
individual duty for every Muslim who can do it in any country in
which it is possible to do it..."

The al-Qaeda attack on a U.S. naval ship called the U.S.S.
Cole off the coast of Aden, Yemen, in October 2000, fulfilled bin
Laden's command. During that attack, a small boat came up to
the side of the American ship. The boat exploded and blew a
hole in the U.S.S. Cole. The attack killed 17 U.S. naval soldiers.
Thirty-nine others were injured.

Never did al-Qaeda members kill more Americans in one
attack than they did on September 11, 2001. On that day, 19
al-Qaeda terrorists hijacked four commercial airplanes in the U.S.
They planned to crash them into American targets on the east
coast. The first two planes crashed into the towers of the World

This photo was taken shortly after the second plane hit the World Trade Center in New York.

Trade Center in New York City. The third one smashed into the Pentagon in Washington, D.C. The fourth plane never found its target. Some of the plane's passengers took control from the hijackers. That plane crashed in a field in Shanksville, Pennsylvania. In all, about 3,000 people died or were missing. These were the worst terrorist attacks on U.S. soil in history.

Currently, there are believed to be al-Qaeda cells in 60 countries worldwide, including the U.S. Al-Qaeda also has relationships with other terrorist organizations. A few of the groups with al-Qaeda connections are al-Jihad, Al-Gamma, and Egyptian Islamic Jihad. Some of the jihad groups are from Sudan, Saudi Arabia, Yemen, Somalia, and Eritrea. They exist in other countries as well.

Most of al-Qaeda's power used to be in Afghanistan. Since the U.S. bombed Afghanistan in late 2001, al-Qaeda forces have moved to other nations around the world.

HAMAS

The word "Hamas" is Arabic for zeal, courage, and bravery. The letters h-a-m-a also stand for Harakat al-Muqawamah al-Islamiyya, or Islamic Resistance Movement. Hamas is a major radical Islamic fundamentalist terrorist organization that began in 1988. It mainly operates out of the Gaza Strip and the West Bank.

Hamas grew out of the Muslim Brotherhood Movement, which began in Egypt in the 1920s. This movement represented an Islamic revival that resulted in branches in over 70 countries. The Muslim Brotherhood Movement's main objectives are to:

- Build the Muslim individual so that each has a strong body, good manners, cultured thought, the ability to earn money, strong faith, correct worship, conscientiousness of time, beneficial to others, organized, and always improving.
- Build the Muslim family by choosing a good wife or husband and by teaching children about Islam.

Israeli-born Sheikh Ahmed Yassin is the founder of the Hamas terrorist group.

- Build the Muslim society by addressing the problems of society realistically.
- Build the Islamic state.
- Build unity between Islamic states.
- Master the world with Islam.

In the 1970s, Sheikh Ahmed Yassin founded the Palestinian branch of the Muslim Brotherhood Movement in the Gaza Strip. Yassin is their spiritual leader known for his fiery personality. For almost 20 years, this branch worked for the Palestinian people. It helped people in mosques, or Islamic places of worship, and clinics. It also did social work. By 1986, this branch directed 40 percent of the mosques in Gaza. It also controlled the Islamic University in Gaza.

For years, the Israeli government secretly supported the Muslim Brotherhood. Israel donated millions of dollars to schools and mosques that were under the leadership of the Palestinian Muslim Brotherhood in Gaza. During this time, the group was dedicated to helping people. It was not involved in violence. Israeli authorities saw the Brotherhood as a better, more peaceful, alternative to the Palestine Liberation Organization (PLO).

The Palestinian people in the West Bank and the Gaza Strip had long felt oppressed by the Israeli government. Israel

Hamas

had claimed its independence in 1948. Since that time, the Israeli government took control of land that once belonged to the Palestinian people. Palestinians felt that the Israeli government aimed for Palestinian submission to Israeli rule.

On December 9, 1987, the Palestinians began a revolt in what would become known as the first intifada, or uprising. Palestinians began to fight against Israeli forces in the occupied territories. The Israeli military responded, and there was a heavy loss of life.

Sheikh Ahmed Yassin was angry about the Israeli government's violent actions. Less than three months later, he changed his organization's name to Hamas. Hamas' goal was to fight a holy war against the Israeli government and create an Islamic state in Israel. Its members took part in street violence and murder to accomplish their goal.

Hamas began violent attacks against Israelis in the late 1980s. In 1989, it kidnapped and killed two Israeli Defense soldiers.

In 1991, Hamas ran two Israeli soldiers over with a van. The group also targeted civilians. Most of Hamas' violent attacks were drive-by shootings, stabbings, and kidnappings. By the mid 1990s, the group's members began using suicide bombings.

On October 19, 1994, a suicide bomber blew himself up on a Tel-Aviv bus. Twenty-two people were killed.

Armed Hamas soldiers take part in an anti-Israeli protest in the Gaza Strip.

More suicide bombings followed. Hamas does not want peace between Israelis and Palestinians. It does not want Israel to exist at all. Some people believe that Hamas attacks may be more damaging to the peace process between Israelis and Palestinians than anything else.

Hamas' goal is jihad against Israelis. It wants Palestine to be freed from Israeli control. It also wants to establish an "Islamic Palestine from the Mediterranean Sea to the Jordan River."

Hamas is strongest in the Palestinian areas of the West Bank and the Gaza strip. Over time it has become stronger and more well known. Some Hamas members are present in Lebanon, Iran, and Syria.

Palestinian expatriates finance Hamas. Expatriates are Palestinians who have been forced from their land. Hamas also receives money from wealthy donors in the Persian Gulf region, especially from Saudi Arabia. Iran also gives Hamas between $20 million and $30 million dollars a year. Some Muslim charities in Europe and the U.S. also work to claim funds for the group.

Sheikh Yassin is now a frail man who is almost blind. He is also confined to a wheelchair. Still, he continues to hold great power among Palestinians.

HEZBOLLAH

Hezbollah is Arabic for "party of God." Hezbollah is also known as Islamic Jihad, Revolutionary Justice Organization, Islamic Jihad for the Liberation of Palestine, and Organization of the Oppressed on Earth. This Lebanon-based group of radical fundamentalists is made up of Shiite Muslims. It formed in 1982.

Israeli forces had invaded Lebanon in 1982. While the Israeli government called this attack the Peace for Galilee War, it was anything but peaceful. This was the second invasion of its kind. The Israeli government's goal both times was to rid Lebanon of the PLO. The fighting from both invasions forced hundreds of thousands of Lebanese from their homes.

During this same period of time, Iran had sent fighters into Lebanon. These fighters were to support Lebanon in a holy war, or jihad, against Israel. This increased Iranian presence in Lebanon, along with Israel's 1982 invasion, led to the creation

Sheikh Hassan Nasrallah, the operations leader of the Hezbollah terrorist group

of Hezbollah. Hezbollah was created to unite Shiite fundamentalists throughout the Middle East.

Sheikh Muhammed Hussein Fadlallah is considered Hezbollah's spiritual father. He was an arbiter, or moral judge, within Lebanon's Shiite community. The current operations leader of Hezbollah is Sheikh Hassan Nasrallah. He joined the Hezbollah movement in its first year of operation. He had been a member of the Shiite Muslim group AMAL before joining Hezbollah. Nasrallah brought many of his faithful followers with him to the Hezbollah movement.

Like Hamas, Hezbollah resents Israel's occupation of Arab land. Members of this group consider Israel the "little Satan." In 1985, Hezbollah published its goals:

- Establish governments to be led by Islamic holy men. (This terrorist group considers Iran's religious government, led by the Ayatollah Khomeini from 1979 to 1989, as its model.)
- Fight against and rid Lebanon of Western rule and influence. (Hezbollah wants to remove all invaders from Muslim nations. In addition to Israel, the U.S. and other Western countries are considered invaders. Some Muslims call the U.S. the "Great Satan.")
- Force Israeli control from Lebanon.

Hezbollah

- Destroy Israel and reclaim the holy city of Jerusalem. (Hezbollah members consider it their religious duty to destroy Israel and free Jerusalem from Israeli control.)

The U.S. State Department reports that Hezbollah gets most of its financial support from Iran. Iran also provides Hezbollah with training, weapons, and explosives. In addition, Hezbollah has received organizational, political, and diplomatic aid from Syria.

Most of Hezbollah's followers live in the Shiite-dominated regions of Lebanon. These include areas in southern Lebanon and parts of Beirut. Many of Hezbollah's members also live in the Bekaa Valley.

Hezbollah has been involved in many terrorist acts against Israel, the U.S., and other Western nations. In the 1980s, the group was involved in a string of kidnappings. Westerners, including Americans, were the targets.

In October of 1983, the terrorist group targeted U.S. buildings in Beirut. Both attacks were suicide truck bombings. One blew up at the U.S. Embassy. The other blew up at the U.S. Marine barracks. The attack on the Marine barracks killed more than 200 U.S. Marines.

Hezbollah members pray in the mountains of Lebanon.

In 1985, Hezbollah hijacked TWA flight 847, which was scheduled to fly from Athens to Rome. One person died during this incident. Three Hezbollah members were put on the FBI's 22 most wanted terrorists list after this hijacking.

Hezbollah has attacked targets worldwide. In 1992, Hezbollah bombed the Israeli Embassy in Argentina. Twenty-nine people were killed. In 1994, the group bombed an Argentinean Jewish community center. The blast killed 95 people.

Hezbollah's terrorist activity grew steadily during the 1990s. In 1991, Hezbollah was responsible for 52 terrorist attacks. That was a sharp climb from the 19 attacks in 1990. Hezbollah took part in 63 attacks in 1992. In 1993, they were responsible for 158 attacks. Hezbollah terrorists carried out 187 attacks in 1994. In 1995, there were 344 attacks. The trend continues.

Since 1990, Syria has controlled Lebanon. Terrorist experts say that without Syria's support Hezbollah could not successfully function within Lebanon. Experts estimate there are several thousand Hezbollah members. They say that since 1992 Hezbollah has become increasingly more powerful in Lebanon's politics.

OTHER MIDDLE EAST TERRORIST GROUPS

In addition to al-Qaeda, Hamas, and Hezbollah, there are other terrorist groups present in the Middle East. Each of them has a specific mission and a plan for attaining their goals. Common among these groups is a hatred for the Jewish state of Israel. Each of them wants to see Israel destroyed. They want Israeli land to be given back to the Palestinian people.

Popular Front for the Liberation of Palestine (PFLP)

One prominent terrorist group in the Middle East today is the Popular Front for the Liberation of Palestine, or PFLP. George Habash founded this radical Islamic fundamentalist group in December 1967, after the Six Day War. The Six Day War resulted in Israel's victory over a number of neighboring Arab countries.

Popular Front for the Liberation of Palestine (PFLP) members burn an Israeli flag.

The PFLP operates in Syria, Lebanon, Israel, the West
Bank, and Gaza. It is determined to establish a democratic
socialist government in the future state of Palestine. Little is
known about how the group is funded. It is known that the
PFLP receives political shelter and is partly managed by Syria.

The PFLP does not agree with the peace talks that PLO
Chairman Yasser Arafat has participated in with Israel. It does
not want to divide Middle East territory into Israeli and
Palestinian lands. The PFLP believes that Palestinians are
entitled to all of Israel.

The PFLP has taken part in many terrorist activities since
the 1970s. It was involved in numerous attacks in Israel during
the 2000s. Some of these have included car bombings in which
civilians were hurt.

Palestine Liberation Front (PLF)

Another terrorist group is the Palestine Liberation Front, or
PLF. This radical Islamic fundamentalist group was created in
1977. Its members had been part of another radical group, the
Popular Front for the Liberation of Palestine-General Command,
or PFLP-GC, before forming the PLF.

When it was formed, Muhammad Zaidan, also known as
Abu Abbas, and Tal'at Ya'akub led the PLF. The organization

split into three smaller groups between 1983 and 1984. Each group kept the name Palestine Liberation Front. Each group believed it represented the original PLF. A different person led each. In 1988, Tal'at Ya'akub died. His group merged with one of the other PLF groups.

The PLF has been responsible for a number of violent attacks. The group led by Abu Abbas is known for carrying out the most visible acts of terrorism. The most famous attack by this group was the 1985 hijacking of the Italian cruise ship *Achille Lauro*. Four PLF terrorists, Bassam al-Askar, Ibrahim Fatayer Abdelatif, Youssef Magied al-Molqi, and Ahmad Marrouf al-Assadi, boarded the ship. Al-Molqi shot and killed a wheelchair-bound tourist. The man and his wheelchair were both thrown overboard. The hijacking ended when the terrorists gave themselves up to Egyptian authorities. The Egyptians allowed the terrorists to fly away on an Egyptian airliner. U.S. fighter jets circled the plane and forced it to land in Italy. All four of the terrorists were tried in an Italian court. All were sentenced to prison.

Zaidan, or Abu Abbas, was found guilty of planning the attack even though he wasn't at the trial. He was wanted by the Italian government for his role in the hijacking. In April 2003, he was captured outside of Baghdad by U.S. forces.

A member of the Abu Nidal Organization in a training camp in Lebanon

Abu Nidal Organization (ANO)

Another well-known Middle East terrorist network is the Abu Nidal Organization, or ANO. The group is also called the Arab Revolutionary Brigade, Black June, or Black September Organization. It is known, too, as the Fatah Revolutionary Council. ANO, made up of radical Islamic fundamentalists, was created in 1974. Abu Nidal, who was also known as Sabri al-Banna, led it. The ANO's goal was to defeat Israel. It wanted to remove Israel from Palestinian lands. The organization was well funded at least until 1987. Until then, ANO received money and military support from Iraq, Libya, and Syria.

From 1974 until 1980, the group was headquartered in Baghdad, Iraq. It carried out many of its missions from Baghdad on behalf of Iraq. These missions included the 1976 attacks on the Syrian embassies in Pakistan and Italy.

Abu Nidal's headquarters moved from Iraq to Syria in the early 1980s. It continued attacking enemy targets. Since the 1990s, the ANO seems to have weakened. Few terrorist activities since then have been linked to them.

OTHER WORLD TERRORIST GROUPS

Terrorists are not unique to the Middle East. There are terrorist groups all over the world.

Chechen Rebels

Among the most notable terrorist groups are the rebels of Chechnya. Generations of Chechens have lived for centuries in the mountains of the former Soviet Union. Most Chechens are Muslim. Through the years, they have resisted Soviet control.

The Soviet Union broke apart in 1991. Several of the republics that made up the Soviet Union declared their independence. The Republic of Chechnya was one of them. It wanted to create an independent Islamic nation.

The Russian government ignored Chechnya's request for independence. The Chechen independence movement resulted. This loosely formed group has been responsible for many terrorist attacks. One of their most recent attacks included a

A Chechen rebel with an assault rifle

takeover of a Moscow theater in October 2002. About 700 people were taken hostage. Many of the terrorists, as well as 129 hostages, died in rescue efforts.

November 17

Not all terrorist groups are based on religious ideals. Some have organized for political reasons. One of these groups is November 17, which is based in Greece. November 17, 1973, marks the day a group of students protested at a University in Athens, Greece. Greek army tanks came to stop the protest. The tanks killed 20 students.

These terrorists, about 25 in number, hate Western nations, especially the U.S. They stand against capitalism, which is the economic system of many Western nations. In capitalist societies, wealth is unevenly divided among the people.

This terrorist group supports communist ideals. Communism is an economic system that is based on the sharing of wealth among all people.

November 17's first known attack occurred in 1975. It has attacked targets for almost 30 years. Since 2002, the Greek government has been effective in cracking down on this group's terrorist activities.

Shining Path

The Shining Path of Peru is another politically motivated terrorist group. It is larger and more violent than November 17. University Professor Abimael Guzman founded it in the late 1960s. The group was created to oppose an unfair, class-based and race-based social system. Its goal was to help the extremely poor, native people of Peru. The group wants to force out the existing Peruvian government. It would like to replace it with a communist government.

The Shining Path was responsible for violent attacks throughout the 1980s and early 1990s. Thousands of people died in attacks by these radicals. The Peruvian government responded fiercely to the Shining Path in the 1990s. It sent thousands of Peruvians to prison for terrorism-related crimes. Many of them received life sentences. This seems to have quieted the Shinning Path. Experts warn, though, that there are still active members of the group. They are believed to be working throughout Peru, trying to recruit new members.

Irish Republican Army (IRA)

The Irish Republican Army, or IRA, was a terrorist group created in 1969. Catholics and Protestants were fighting in Ireland. British troops came in to help. Many Catholics felt that British troops handled the situation unfairly. They felt that the British favored the Protestants. As a result, many Irish Catholics put their faith in the IRA to fight injustices.

An Irish Republic Army, IRA, member with a missile launcher

The IRA's goal was to unite Ireland and remove British control in Northern Ireland. It fought injustice in Ireland through bloody terrorist attacks. Since the late 1960s, the IRA has killed about 1,800 people. About 650 of those were civilians. The group targeted ordinary people. It bombed bars and subway stations.

In recent years, the IRA has changed its focus. In 1998, most of Northern Ireland's political parties signed the Good Friday Agreement. The IRA and other groups who signed it promised to reduce violence. As of late 2000, the U.S. State Department said it no longer considered the IRA a terrorist group. The IRA began to reduce its weapons supply in 2001.

Conclusion

Terrorist groups can be motivated by religion or politics. Each group believes that it represents the oppressed. At the same time, each group causes great pain to ordinary citizens who bear no responsibility for the group's suffering.

It has been said that what one person calls a terrorist another may call a freedom fighter. The terrorist groups described in this book likely consider themselves freedom fighters. Those who experience and witness the groups' violence, though, probably believe the term "terrorist" is quite accurate.

TERRORIST GROUPS

WEB SITES
WWW.ABDOPUB.COM

Would you like to learn more about Terrorist Groups? Please visit www.abdopub.com to find up-to-date Web site links about Terrorist Groups and the World in Conflict. These links are routinely monitored and updated to provide the most current information available.

A poster in a New York storefront after the September 11 terrorist attacks

TIMELINE

Late 1920s Muslim Brotherhood Movement begins in Egypt.

1967 The Popular Front for the Liberation of Palestine is founded.

1970s The Palestinian branch of the Muslim Brotherhood is founded.

1974 The Abu Nidal Organization is formed.

1977 The Palestine Liberation Front is created.

1979 The Soviets invade Afghanistan. The mujahedeen, or Islamic holy warriors, are recruited to defend Afghanistan.

1982 Hezbollah is formed.

1987 Palestinians revolt against Israeli control. This is called the first intifada.

1988 Osama bin Laden's followers take the name al-Qaeda. Hamas begins operations.

1989 The mujahedeen, with the help of the U.S. government, force the last of the Soviets from Afghanistan.

2001 Al-Qaeda terrorists attack U.S. targets on September 11.

2003 Muhammad Zaidan, or Abu Abbas, is captured by U.S. forces outside Baghdad, Iraq.

FAST FACTS

- The word "terrorism" was first coined in France in the late eighteenth century.
- The FBI did not begin to formally track annual terrorism data until the mid-1970s.
- During the Soviet invasion of Afghanistan, both Osama bin Laden and the U.S. supported Afghanistan.
- The following countries are considered sponsors of terrorism: Iran, Iraq, Syria, Libya, Cuba, North Korea, and Sudan.
- The U.S. government blamed the September 11, 2001, terrorist attacks on Osama bin Laden and other radical Islamic fundamentalists. Bin Laden and other radical Islamic fundamentalists blame the attacks on the arrogance of the U.S. government.
- Terrorist groups that are motivated by religious concerns are becoming more common.
- The U.S. State Department sets and maintains U.S. foreign policy.
- In response to the September 11, 2001 attacks, President George W. Bush established the U.S. Department of Homeland Security. Tom Ridge heads this department. One of the department's main roles is to educate the public about how to prepare for an emergency, including a possible terrorist attack.

GLOSSARY

Afghanistan:

A landlocked country in the Middle East.

AMAL (Afwaj al Muqawama al Lubnaniya):

A military organization representing the Shiite Muslims of Lebanon.

barracks:

A building or group of buildings used to house military personnel.

Belfast:

Capital and largest city of Northern Ireland; the center of Irish Protestantism.

Catholic:

A Christian denomination.

civilian:

A person who is not an active member of the military or police.

hijack:

To overtake a vehicle, such as an airplane, by threatening the pilot or driver with violence.

Islam:

The religion of Muslims. It is based on the teachings of the Prophet Muhammad.

TERRORIST GROUPS

Islamic fundamentalist:

A Muslim believer who strictly observes what is written in the Muslim holy book, which is called the Koran.

liberation:

The act of setting something or someone free.

occupied territories:

Territory occupied, or controlled, by Israel.

Palestine:

A region in Middle East that was once controlled by Arabs.

Protestant:

A member of a Western Christian church who is not Catholic.

Sheikh:

An Islamic religious leader.

Shiite Muslim:

A member of the branch of Islam that regards Ali and his descendants as the legitimate successors to the Prophet Muhammad.

Soviet Union:

The largest, most powerful, communist country until 1991.

Sunni Muslim:

The original Sunni Muslims believed that they should vote for the Prophet Muhammad's successor.

Western nation:

A country in the western hemisphere that is predominantly Christian.

INDEX